Facing Mount Kenya,

a Running Commentary

Najar Nyakio Munyinyi

Lens&Pens Publication, LLC

Auburn, WA

ISBN: 9780998920023

Cover design, layout, and Authoress Photograph by Nala Ayieta (The pH) Instagram @nalaayieta nalaayieta@gmail.com

AUTHORESS NOTE

I first wrote then published on-line this critique in 2017. It was widely read and circulated.

it is now September of 2022 – why would I want to re-publish it physically?

September in Africa is a beginning of a New Year, and this particular season began with the Death of the Queen of Elizabeth II. An immediate outpouring of rage among both the black and white communities regarding her colonial brutality ricocheted across the world. Many countries in the "commonwealth" have re-fused to sign fusing pacts with her drunken son Charles.

There is a clarion call for Africans in the diaspora and especially on the continent to begin the work of re-form and a re-structuring of ancient trade routes, and re-construct ancestral trading patterns.

When I spoke to Skeeter - a wonderful human being who has published in the USA - to assist me in the publishing of this booklet, (it cannot be published in Nairobi as "we're not quite there yet") he responded, "yes, but please, manage your expectations".

I have no expectations beyond the desire to state that "these words have been formally put down on paper and printed" and read by you, dear reader. Once you read the information there-in, return here, and respond to this question.

Q: Now that you have this knowledge, what now is the way forward?

Answer from me is that as Africans continent-wide, and as "Kenyans" in this part of the world, we need to rethink whom we are, and moreover, to re-consider and re-structure our land issues. Further, we have not been allowed to speak of ourselves as mwana' inchi, as women, as ordinary "Kenyans" – only the Professors and the "learned" were allowed to bring to us laws learned from foreign lands and institutions therein. Only professors were allowed to tell a foreign tale.

The commoner was not allowed tell their stories nor criticize the colonizers branding. We had been dis-membered, and now we are re-membering. We are now putting together our his and shestories, ideas, cultures, habits, practices and all those things that had been pulled and fallen apart.

Tell your story, fearlessly! Sing it, Write poetry, write a booklet, dance your story, act it out in Drama – choose a medium, and tell your African Story.

~ Maaitu Najar Nyakio

CONTENTS

FORWARD

Najar Nyakio is an African she-warrior. She has a very strong core and sense of purpose. It comes from within. Her pursuit of these topics is far more meaningful than anything I could or should engage in as an outsider to her culture. I have grown to admire her strength as a human and her relentless pursuit of justice. Though I have yet to meet her, I consider her to be my sister both in our commitment to our faith and our desire for a truly just world.

In this book she challenges the narratives of the past, especially as described in Kenyatta's book *Facing Mount Kenya.* It is always important to challenge common narratives of the past. This is a critical part of the journey to understanding.

During my graduate studies, I interviewed elders throughout the Gikuyu highlands. Early on I would quote *Facing Mount Kenya* as a segue to a conversation. Often the elders would dismissively wave Kenyatta's book aside. He, they would say, was not raised among the Agikuyu. His book, in their view, was, at best misleading. Nyakio pushes this concept further to uncover the darker motives for the narrative Kenyatta gave in his work about the Gikuyu.

She also argues for an integrated African conscience. This same argument is made by other African thinkers. In my studies I found a numbers of unifying factors that extend far beyond "tribe." This amalgamated Africa was taught to children at an early age.

For example; There is a traditional story told by grandparents to their children in the traditional Gikuyu world. The same story is retold in different ways by almost every culture in Kenya and in southern Africa.

The basic story begins with a father who had three sons who did not get along with each other and their brawls often escalated into fighting. The father petitioned the Creator for guidance. The father was told to lay three items at the feet of his sons and tell them to choose an Item. In the Gikuyu version, the first son picked up a spear. "You," the Creator said, "Will be the father of the Maasai, warriors and keepers of cattle." The second son picked up a bow. "You", the Creator said, "Will be the father of the N'Dorobo, hunters of wild animals." The third son picked up a digging stick. "You," the Creator said, "Will be the father of the Gikuyu, the farmers of the land."

When this story was told, the storyteller would instruct the meaning; There may be differences between the Gikuyu and her neighbors but in the end, neighboring peoples are family, too. The terms "tribe" and "tribal" are concepts imposed on Africa from the slave traders and colonial overlords. The true relationships between sub-cultures were far more in keeping with the philosophy variously described as Ubuntu—where there is no division between the individual and all of humanity.

Nyakio, in this book, strips away the Western Imposed hierarchy of race and civilization—an underlining premise of *Facing Mount Kenya*, and returns it back to the older African unifying philosophy. In doing so she has given a starting point for understanding the pre-colonial concepts of African

Civilization from an African's perspective.

The very idea of tribe or tribal comes from the vocabulary of Western anthropology in which societies are described in terms of social complexity. The simplest social structures are called "social bands," then tribes, chieftains, and the "progress" of complexity continues until it is encompassed in the term, "state." In the post-modern era even the idea of "state" is being challenged in preference for the next level of complexity.

The historical setting in which the hierarchy of social complexity was born, is the same era that gave birth to the idea of a hierarchy of races—putting "whiteness" on top, and "blackness" on the bottom. Racial hierarchy became the justification of slavery, the elevation of the races, and the horrors of the "science of eugenics."

The hierarchy of social complexity has taken on a similar imperative to lift the "lower" social orders of "less complex" civilizations and lead them (most often by coercion) to the "more sophisticated" level of the "state."

When Africa allows for itself the terminology of "tribes" they knowingly or unknowingly align themselves with nineteenth century ideas of Western Civilization. The West (in its imagination) being the ultimate achievement of human complexity.

What this all ignores is that Africa—and it is not alone in this—historically achieved its own complexity without the onerous burden of a state complex. It was - and still is - an amazingly complex civilization which is able to have different cultures and languages co-exist in both their unique diversity, and also, under the umbrella of the Ubuntu philosophy that connects a unified humanity in the midst of a complex diversity.

This is an amazingly complex achievement in civilization. It accomplished this with a united humanity philosophically, rather than, as in the west, by the force of law.

Africa had and has achieved what Western Civilization has only been able to achieve by force—one of the several reasons that Western Civilization is based in violence.

Some of Nyakio's points are very challenging to me as a historian. Others I also discovered. I can only hope that many among the Gikuyu people will find Nyakio's work to be equally challenging to their own self-perception. As a thinker and a she-warrior, Nyakio is equal to those challenges. I truly believe that this book becomes another gateway for dialogue among the Agikuyu, all Kenyans, and Africans everywhere.

Skeeter Wilson, African Historian and Author of *Crossing Rivers* and *Take Nothing With You.*

INTRO

When I first read *Facing Mount Kenya* by Jomo Kenyatta, I was in distress, for it was pretty clear to me that the culture Jomo Kenyatta wrote about was based on treachery, not only against a peoples, or against earth - (the land and environment) - it was a book that arrogantly dismissed the female. I had found the book in my Father's library as a curious 11-year-old, but even then it did not sit right with me, for I had listened well to the stories told to me first by my paternal great-grandmother and later, my grandfather. There were also strange oddities that I could not quite put my young fingers on, so I set it aside and began to delve deeper into whom I was, as a Kenyan, as an African, as a Female, and as a member of the Kikuyu Tribe. I have read hundreds of other books, explored his thesis, discussed and studied the issues I write about below with countless men and women from the Kikuyu tribe, and listened and to many *non*-Kikuyu, Kenyan men, and women.

Years later I am confident and unapologetic enough to use his book to prove that Kenyatta and his writers (or could it be that the authors manipulated Kenyatta deliberately? You decide after this) - used "Facing Mount Kenya" as *the* key anthropological thesis on which the culture of the Kikuyu tribe may gain its' insights. But not only that, the book was used to wipe out and conceal the real history of Kenyans - specifically the Maasai Kingdom and the people of Ma'at.

Was this book written to hide our royal line ancestries from the Kingdom of Axum (Aksum)? What I know is that the Black African Swahili Empire has one of the greatest and oldest histories worldwide, and that Kenyans are *not* different tribes, but one people. *Facing Mount Kenya* was written to *establish* a new race of people called the **Agi-kuyu** whose roots are intricately tied in and *knotted* with the Europeans – a foreign race that came into Kenya to dominate it for its resources. But in order to do this they had to break down and disrupt the dominant tribes who lived in what is popularly referred to as the Kenyan or White Highlands – the *Maasai* or the *People of Ma'at* had to *'go'*. Secondly, the British had to implant and instill pseudo-clones for the continuation of the extraction of the resources that are found within these lands.

But I'm moving too fast - I think…

Let me come "srowry…" (as we say in Kenyanese)

PART I

i. Whitewashing Kenya's Real History

First, let us understand how this book came into being from a man who was not a born writer but whose career began as a parking ticket clerk.

Jomo Kenyatta was born between 1891 and 1897 when East Africa was in the control of the Imperial British East Africa Company (IBEAC) - a trading company whose top agenda was profiteering. IBEAC was the administrator of British East Africa which was the forerunner of the East African Protectorate and later yet, Kenya. The IBEAC was a commercial association founded to cultivate trade in the areas controlled by British colonial power. Created after the Berlin Treaty of 1885, which brutally annexed and divvied up Africa rather like a Pizza Inn pizza - IBEAC was led by that most awful of men, William MacKinnon, who built upon his company's trading activities in the region with the encouragement of the British government through the granting of "imperial charter" — although it remains unclear what this actually meant, but, it "granted immunity of *prosecution* to British Subjects whilst allowing them the right to raise taxes, impose custom duties, administer justice, make treaties and otherwise act as the authority of the area. (Oliver, Roland (March 1951). "Some Factors in the British Occupation of East Africa, 1884 - 1894" In other words, in the History of Kenya, despite the murders of millions of

Kenyans, only *one* white man was ever persecuted and given the capital punishment for the deliberate killing of an African.

"The British subjects, have immunity of prosecution." To Date.

Before the conference, European *mercenaries* and *missionaries* who were in truth undercover mercenaries, treated African indigenous people in the same contemptuous manner as they had done the New World Natives - by forming *trading* relationships with indigenous chiefs. In the early 1800's, the search for ivory in Africa which was then often used in the production of luxurious products like piano keys, jewelry, cutlery, chopsticks and included dentures - led many white traders further into the interior of Africa. However, with the exception of trading posts along the coasts, the greater interior of the continent was essentially ignored during this period. (Muriel E. Chamberlain, *The Scramble for Africa* (1999).) IBEA was a conglomerate that did not *care* about the humanity of the East African *peoples*. Our ancestors existed as commodities of profit - either as beasts of burden, laborers, or curiosities collected for study in Scientific Zoos. All servants and slaves born were noted in the diaries of the administration and each had a price on his head – this then, was imperial privilege.

ii. Before Facing Mount Kenya

While in his early thirties, Johnstone Kamau joined the Kikuyu Central Association (KCA), a political organization that strove to make the British administrators in Kenya understand colonialism's destructive impact *specifically* on the Kikuyu people. (Shaw 1995). In particular, the KCA raised attention for the grievances caused by land alienation for in their eyes, as long as the Europeans continued to grab what they called '*Kikuyu Lands*', the KCA argued that the *Kikuyu* would be unable to develop into self-governing modern subjects.

However, being racially ethnic based and founded on patriarchal philosophies, the KCA Koc's (Kikuyu's Only Club) did not have much impact within the colony itself as the Kikuyu tribe was a *minority* within the protectorate. Kenyatta's interest in politics only began from his friendship with James Beauttah, a senior figure in KCA and one of the founders. Beauttah took Kenyatta to a political meeting in Pumwani (a municipality within Nairobi City) but, afraid to disrupt his lucrative employment, Kenyatta refused to make a commitment to the organization. Meanwhile, political upheavals occurred across Kikuyu land following World War I. Among these demonstrations against the British Empire were the campaigns of the brilliant Harry Thuku and the East African Association which resulted in the British government massacre of 21 Native protesters in March 1922. Kenyatta though, was visibly absent.

In either 1925 or early 1926, Beauttah moved to Uganda. When the KCA wrote to Beauttah and asked him to travel to London as their representative, he declined, but recommended Kenyatta—who had 'a good command of English'—to go in his stead. Kenyatta accepted on the condition that the Association matched his pre-existing wages, which they did, and voilà, Kenyatta thus became the group's secretary and shipped himself off to London.

In London he initially sought shelter with the Scottish

missionaries for their ways were familiar to him, but the same predicaments that had dogged him in Kenya soon followed in London. His troubles began when the missionaries completely withdrew their support once they learned about Johnstone Kamau's sexual relations with European women outside of marriage, his communist sentiments and his habitual drunkenness. (Ibid.). The mission societies within Kenya had also begun to take a firm stance against Kikuyu female circumcision, which Johnstone Kamau was violently against as he advocated pungently for female circumcision. (Berman 1996: 318-319).

Homeless in London, Kamau subsequently went bowl-begging and reached a compromise with liberal imperialists, who introduced him to the British Education system "…in order to improve his language skills..". However, he realized that the liberal imperialists were only primarily concerned with extending British colonial power into Kikuyu land and understood that his agenda and their plans were irreconcilable (Ibid.: 320). Finally, though, at 45 years of age, his windfall changed for the better when he met Bronislaw Malinowksi in December of 1934.

iii. About The Russian, Bronislaw Malinowksi

A sector of East Africa's population had long fascinated the anthropologist Malinowski specifically because of their fierce rejection of Christianity based on the principal that they had their own indigenous cultures which were based on an intricate system of philosophies and beliefs. Malinowski had tried often to organize a fieldwork programme in Kenya to study different tribes, but he had never managed to pull it off. Now that Johnstone Kamau was in London, Malinowski jumped on an opportunity – in short shrift, Johnstone Kamu was enrolled in the department of Social Anthropology at the London School of Economics where Prof. Malinowski taught. Soon, an intimate pupil-instructor relation formed between the pair. At the end of his Studies at the London School of Economics, Johnstone Kamau wrote a thesis in which he propagated Kikuyu customs and traditions as fact. He used the names Jomo Kenyatta, Jomo meaning the sound akin to when withdrawing a sword from its sheath, and *Kinyatta*, the Kikuyu name of a belt worn by *Maasai.*

Thus, *Facing Mount Kenya*, by Jomo Kenyatta, was born.

The book was an edited version of the thesis which became 'one of the first modern ethnographies written by an African'. Malionwski had achieved his objective! Both Jomo and Malinowski had very large stakes in having the thesis work accepted as academically 'pure' and 'value-neutral' (see Pels 1999: 109), but in truth, Jomo was not a writer and at 45 was more interested in politics and less in anthropology. His aim was largely to maintain what he called 'Kikuyu Lands within a Kikuyu Majority' – the freedom of other peoples of Kenya from colonial rule was never a part of his ambition.

At the time, Malinowski praised Jomo's work for its lack of political purpose and its "scientificity" but in reality, Facing Mount Kenya was not at all written 'without any passion or feeling' and it certainly did not present the facts objectively – it was a political manifesto against British imperialism in 'Kikuyu Lands', masqueraded as a cultural historical analysis. (Akker, M.L. van den Title: Monument of Nature, An ethnography of the World Heritage of Mt. Kenya Issue Date: 2016-05-25)

PART II

Set in an obscure fable timeframe, Kenyatta wrote that once upon a time, *Gikuyu* was given a beautiful wife named **Moombi** which in Utu (the language of the Bantu) means **Creator** or **Moulder**. They settled in a place known as *Mokorwe wa Nyagathanga* which means "the place of fig trees". A "*mukuyu*" is a species of wild fig tree. A "*gikuyu*" is a *giant* or very old wild fig tree. The Kikuyu declare that the bird species '*nyagathanga'*, is an 'unknown bird'. According to this thesis, *Gikuyu* treated his wife well enough, and he is an example in Kikuyu folklore of what a true man ought to be.

Gikuyu and Moombi had 10 daughters, and as the legend goes, 9 young "handsome" men from distant lands were found and approved to marry the daughters of this founding family. Only 9 daughters were married as the 10th elected to remain single and set apart as a Seer, Aunty – the Eccentric Older Sister. Her primary functions were to care for the health of the entire clan and her home was the home of all her sisters children. Further, her knowledge field was devoted to healing herbs, plants, and the dissemination of medicaments.

i. Against the SisterHood

A few 130 years later (after the death of ***Gikuyu*** and ***Moombi***) these foreign sons-in-law had a sit down, and here we commence to see a problem that begins first with land inheritance, for the 10 daughters are the ones who were the inheritors of land, as prescribed by **Mogai**. The men were the strangers to the land.

> "When *Gikuyu* and *Moombi* died, their daughters inherited their movable and immovable property which they shared equally among them" - 'them' meaning the Sisters. It is written so, and despite the fact that these Sisters were in charge of a stable society, the foreign men went against their dead parents-in-laws rule-of-law.
>
> "…. It is *said* that while holding a superior position in the community, the women became domineering and ruthless fighters. They also practiced polyandry. And, through sexual jealousy, many men were put to death for committing adultery or other minor offences. Besides the capital punishment, the men were subject to all kinds of humiliations and injustice. Men were indignant at the way in which the women treated them, and in their indignation they planned to revolt against the women's administration of justice. But as the women were physically stronger than the men of that time, and also better fighters, it was decided that the best time for a successful revolt would be during the time when the majority of women especially their leaders, were in pregnancy."

This is just page 6 of a thesis. I'm not making this stuff up.

The anger is palpable. Johnstone Kamau aka Jomo Kenyatta, was a furious author: -

"…yet at the beginning, **Mogai** told *Gikuyu* that whenever he was in need, he should make a sacrifice and raise his hands towards *Kere-Nyaga* or the *Mountain of Mystery*, and the **Lord of Nature** will come to his assistance"

Gikuyu's son's in laws and the male grandchildren born of these unions thought otherwise on the raising of hands, on the issue of sacrifice, or of facing *Kere-Nyaga* and requesting for help from the Lord of Nature. They broke the rules and laws they found in these lands and took matters into their own hands – a matter which later proved to be disastrous.

"… the decision was hailed by the men who were very anxious to overthrow the rule of the opposite sex…" Note that **Moombi** is now not called as **Mogai** called her – '**Creator** and **Moulder'** but as an 'opposite'– an – 'other' which translates as 'conflicting, contradictory and contrary'. These names were meant to degenerate her entire being, for a woman gives of herself both the physical and spiritual self.

Rather than the Kikuyu men being 'thankful' towards the kind treatment from their parents in-law and the daughters or turning to **Mogai** as *Gikuyu* the founder of the tribe had been ordered to do by **Mogai** himself, the men turned ugly and jealous. The society had been polyandrous, and the men themselves were allowed to form unions with any woman they so wished. In many of the cultural traditions across this land, the planting of a Man's Spear outside a woman's hut meant that nobody, not even her "husband" was allowed to enter that hut. So where did this word "Polyandry" originate from? This was the custom of the land and for over many years, they were comfortable with their new laws. Remember too, that none of the son-in-laws were the blood of either Gikuyu and **Moombi**, but 'handsome strangers' who were welcomed and requested to marry the daughters. In truth, these son-in-laws wanted the lands and material property that had been given to their wives, for themselves.

ii. Derogatory name-calling & The Beginning of a Curse*

(*A curse is not just to "throw words". It is an actionable deed where the receiver receives no settlement, peace or stability in life – it is being "separate from contentment" and is the "creation of pain".)

In order to deprive or steal from a good and moral person there is a practice known as demoralization. Always the person that you want to steal from is first de-humanized. The disparaging effect is a psychological tool practiced during colonization and slavery - which are the exact same methodology known as capitalism, for capitalism cannot exist outside of either colonialism or slavery, it is a symbiotic relationship - and consists of turning a person into an 'other' – an 'object' – a 'thing'. A derogatory name. The real curse of using demeaning words is that the victim can start to believe that they are fundamentally wrong. They can start to believe that they have less value in the society than the person who is slurring their names. In other words, a victims' very sense of self is shattered by the words and actions of others. Once shattered, it is easy to further degrade them, and once degraded, they do not have the moral energy to rebuild themselves.

iii. The Kikuyu male and the Kenyan man

Has the male culture of a single tribe spilled over from a small section to an entire country? Yes, for in many ethnic groupings around Kenya, men are more often than not, gentle towards their feminine forms, embrace the woman and encourage her activities.

Yet today in the cities of Kenya many, both male and female, have noted with concern that the Kenyan man has begun to 'describe' himself in the terms of the world, by a certain 'kikuyu-ness'. He is ridiculed by the Kikuyu man if he shows affinity towards his females and while it rubs off on many non-kikuyu males as offensive, it has alas, been named as the epitome of Kenyan man through peer pressure, nonstop publicity, literature, and 'advertising'. *The Kikuyu Man is a brand.*

When they get together many men often resort to (name-calling) their **Moombies** as 'slay queens, bitches' or 'the opposite sex', etc. (Yet away from the city, women are honored and treated gently). This tactic announces in a dishonest format that 'women are not only inferior to men, but that in their inferior-ness, they are in competition to men', and that this 'competition' is not welcomed by the men. In other words, *dare raise above me and I shall beat you down* – this messaging is conveyed to women in Kenya daily. Do not best the man in education, achievement, accomplishments, *anything at all.* It is taken as "completion". Women are informed daily that their very natural independence and all biological giftings given to them by **Mogai** is wicked, sinful, and iniquitous.

iv. Things Fall Apart

From page 7 of *Facing Mount Kenya*, the political narrative has already been introduced and readers can begin to decipher how 'things fall apart' within the Kikuyu Society, for in his story Jomo Kenyatta unwittingly leads us to some political truths of this tribe, to the character and to the personality of the Kikuyu male.

> "...the decision was hailed by the men who were very anxious to overthrow the rule of the opposite sex. At once the men held a secret meeting in which they arranged a suitable date to execute their plan. On the day appointed to carry out the initial stage of the revolt, the men started to act enthusiastically. They embarked on a campaign to induce the women leaders and a majority of their brave followers to have sexual intercourse with them. The women were unfortunately deceived by the flattery of the men, and blindly agreed to their inducements without knowing the wicked plans the men had made to overthrow the women's rule. The men, after completing the first act, quietly waited for the results. After six moons had elapsed the men then saw clearly that their plan had materialized. At once they organized into groups and finally carried out the revolt without much resistance. For the brave women were almost paralyzed by the condition in which they were. The men triumphed, took over the leadership in the community and became the heads of their families instead of the women. Immediately steps were taken to abolish the system of polyandry and to establish the system of polygamy..."

The Curse of A Role Reversal

> "The men also decided to change the original name of their tribe, as well as the names of the clans which were given under the matriarchal system to new ones under the patriarchal system. They succeeded in changing the name of the tribe from *Rorerer wa Mbari ya Moombi* to *Rorerer wa Gikuyu* (i.e., *Gikuyu nation or the Children of Gikuyu*). But when it came to the changing of the clan names, the women were very infuriated and strongly decided against the change, which they looked upon as a sign of ingratitude on the part of the men. The women frankly told the men that if they dared to eliminate the names which stood as a recognition that the women were the original founders of the clan system, the women would *refuse* to bear any more children. And to start with, they

> would kill all the male children who were born as a result of the treacherous plan of the revolt.."

I have read many a book on anthropology, and this one is particularly strange. What I did not know at 11 and what I know now is that Jomo wrote it more as a political argument that early on begins with the negation of the Kenyan female. Jomo Kenyatta wrote this book in his 45th year, and nobody was or has been allowed to critique it – well, no one in Kenya (for the book has been banned in Ireland) and no female of this "tribe". Critiques were called dissidents and traitors, kidnapped, tortured, and assassinated. Many writers fled Kenya after – and it has therefore been forced on a Kikuyu population and the world at large at its face value for over 80 years.

PART III

i. Dismantling African Myths

The Kikuyu have existed as a tribe for a maximum of about 100 years. They are a small tribe, but as I shall try to explain, the traditions that Jomo Kenyatta wrote in *Facing Mount Kenya* allows for an '*eating of other communities*' in order for the 'Tribe' to amass land, their primary objective, and to increase population numbers. This is why many Kikuyu, do not '*look Kikuyu*' – these have been *assimilated* into the Kikuyu tribe.

There are particular identifying marker traits in our people and those who have been schooled in the classification of family trees note three features – the eyes and eyebrow shapes, nose and hand shape and length. Other markers are ears and height. These markers are genetic and point to the ancestral origins of each individual. All tribes outside of the Kikuyu have these specific markers. However, the Kikuyu's carry ALL THE MARKERS of those around them due to their 'eating of tribes' principle of assimilation. If they want your land, they will marry into your family.

As Kenyatta himself prefaces in his book, "…the usual European way of spelling this word is "Kikuyu" which is incorrect as it should be *Gikuyu* or in the strict phonetic spelling, *Gokoyo*. This form refers only to the country itself. A *Gikuyu* person is Mu Gi Ku Yu or in plural a Gi Ku Yu.

The older, more ancient group name was ***Moombi***. When searching for the existence of a people, historians often use the science of etymology.

Moombi is M-B-Y, for the **Utu** language consisted mainly of consonants as vowels were introduced by the European. When we talk of the people of Africa, the word **bantu** refers not a '*category* of tribe' but means people – B-T-U = Bantu - wa-tu – w-t-u - utu).

(https://www.youtube.com/watch?v=WczO0q3ALqc&list=PLD4Q_VTKAamOZbrpmln4LST0OHwTGCmXi)

African's have never perceived themselves in terms of separate 'tribes' but in terms of a fluid movement of Utu – *People.* The terms Nilotic, Cushite, Bantu was introduced by the European in an effort to contain and compress the Africans into a 'box' – in today's slang, we would say, '*amewekwa box'* – this is essentially what happened to East Africans. We were diced up and placed into little boxes.

Jomo Kenyatta said so himself, that ".... culture has no meaning apart from the social organization of life on which it is built...". Culture has no meaning AWAY from the social organization of the life on which it is built – whether he came upon this anthropological conclusion by himself, or it was written by Professor Malionwski can be debated upon, but the modern anthropologist knows this as truth. Culture is what holds Africans together and our culture is tied not only to humans, but to the lands, the waters, the hills, mountains (the earth) and all that swims (in the waters) walks, crawls, flies and grows within her sphere/realm or domain.

Without a culture, there is no "living" – or life.

Kenyans today face a grim life with many youth stating that they have no 'life – that "life is meaningless", or that "I cannot afford a life.." – the adages are many, and the reason for this is a complete *cultural* breakdown and a general cognitive dissonance that refuses to accept facts as presented. So deeply wedged and compressed are the untruths about whom we are as Kenyans that truth does not easily trickle to the surface. The older psychologists are at a loss, having obtained Degrees from the same system that teaches a veneration of the white man, his theories and a diminishing of African practicality.

In fact, it has been established that many University institutions are the most institutionalized programs – especially when one dares present views or write a thesis that is outside of the accepted parameters. Any material that is contra to, or controversial to the universities views or outlook is frowned upon. Thus, those who are Africa's "intellectuals" – the Scientists, Doctors and Psychologists are often at a loss - mimicking their European counterparts in trying to treat Mental unease which is as a result of the very social lies that have been told to us, and that continue being replicated to us – that Black or African, is vile, daft, uncivilized and has no history.

This is just a tip of the ice-burg, for universities also morph Black bright youngers into a coon clique that is unable to understand the needs of their greater black sisters and brothers – what they call their poor "dumb cousins", or "village relatives". University education and intellectualism elevates the learned into an Elite alliance all of its own that rarely returns itself to the problems of the masses.

I once spoke to a bitter old pastoralist man in the heart of an Isiolo conservancy who said that "… not having proper schools in the marginalized areas separates us from our children and destroys our cultures – they go to Nairobi to learn, living with aunts and uncles who may not treat them well, but in those expensive schools, they forget about the cows and camels. By the time they are finished with this education, they know nothing about their *culture* and nothing about their *landscape.* They become technically useless which leads both us and them into a relationship of loathsome bitterness…"

The good news is that a younger more literate generation that has access to millions of files of knowledge online has, in an effort to understand the historical ills that have dodged them, gone backwards into our rich and deep African history to try and understand societal issues, finding that most are caused by two factors; a complete breakdown of our cultures, and the subsequent imprudent adoption of foreign 'life-styles' which, like pain medication, do not address the core issues but simply dull the agony.

ii. Africa is a continent of one Bantu. There is nothing like 'Tribe'.

We are not divided into 'tribes, religions, or regions'. This has been the sham all along - we are all one peoples with different skin tones, different heights, different noses, different weights, different eye shapes, and different *hair types.* Africa is a continent of *one* Bantu. Including the Kikuyu, as vile as their history is.

> "When the European comes to the country and robs the people of their land, the white is taking away not only their

> livelihood, but the quantifiable symbol that holds family together. In doing this he gives blows, and these blows cut away at the foundations from the whole of *Gikuyu* life - social, moral, and economic. When the European explains to his own satisfaction and after the most superficial glance at the issues involved, that he is doing this for the *sake of the Africans*, to *civilize* them, to *teach them the disciplinary value of regular work*, and *give them the benefit of European progressive ideas*, he is adding insult to injury, and convinces no one but himself." (Adapted, Jomo Kenyatta 1938: 305)

Jomo Kenyatta was sly, and he understood what the European and the British had come to do in Africa. At first one is suitably excited when he denounces the Scottish Mission and Christian Theology – then one becomes puzzled when hc expects his subjects to shift back to the very ideology that he himself had rejected. The Church became one of the strongest sectors of the State, dictating to Mzee Kenyatta, and to all Kenyans, the political direction of the entire nation. BUT take note of the fact that while he was not unique in talking about the British and the European in general making land claims through a narrative of historical affiliation, his deception was that he addressed a single '*tribe*', and thus contradicted himself at every turn. And this is the problem with Kenya today.

Political freedom, land ownership and citizen privileges do not benefit Kenyans. These benefits have historically aided and still advance the Kikuyu Catholic *first*, then the Kikuyu Christian second. It is an example of the frequent inconsistencies and incongruences tossed out by the Late Founding Father, for Johnstone Kamau was *raised* by the Scottish Missionaries – who are not Catholic, but High Anglican (yet another division within the Christian Church).

This is why I stated and keep repeating that this book and the contradictions in Kenyatta's life are deliberate, to further obscure and muddy his, and the kikuyu's already ambiguous history.

From roughly the late 1920s onwards the British colonial administration was continuously confronted by groups of people asserting their land rights across Kenya on the basis of cultural histories (Lonsdale 2008: 307). But the British had no time nor sympathy with this narrative for they had come to extract wealth. Thus, they alienated and separated people away from themselves – they divided east African "subjects" away from the fluid (always moving and resettling) Utu movements into dense and "Exclusive Tribal" sections of their creation at their whim. They forbade locals to plant cotton or tobacco, they declared '*mavaki*', marijuana and locally made brews *illegal.* They uprooted Arrow-Roots and poisoned streams and wells. They forbade the Kikuyu in particular, to produce Iron, for the Gumba are brilliant metallurgists. The British set huts on fire and killed women and children, again, at whim. They initiated hunting bans, forbade the 'African' from carrying guns in his own land, forbade men to gather wild honey from their own forests. They put up boundaries, declared No Go Zones for other areas.

Exclusive Tribal contracts were often concealed from the people. They were also secretive - deliberate negotiations and manipulations of tribal identities by colonial administrators, and in many cases, by Africans themselves. (see for instance Hamilton 1998; Pels 1996). One of these *coon* Africans was Jomo Kenyatta and is the reason why he wrote a book about a tribe that had never in reality, existed. This division was based on what the white administrators, white missionaries and white anthropologists forced on the people *as cultural markers*, despite the people's refusal, and it paved the way for a distinct colonial geography of native "reserves" that assumed and forced a connection between culture and present physical territory. Understand, there was immense freedom of Utu movement up until the Berlin Conference when it was outrageously shut down.

To this day, those reserves, reservations, or physical land-locked prisons exist and *remain*. Today they are branded as 'Counties'. They used to be known as Reservations or Reserves – the 'Kikuyu' Reserve, the Akamba Reserve, The Meru Reserve, etc. Our cultures have stagnated, we have been locked, on land. This word Reserve is the same word applied to the North American Native population, to the Mexican Indian populations and to the lands owned by the Canadian Indigenous populations. They too are STILL locked in in these Reserves, like living cattle in a very large pen.

iii. Of the Ashkinazi Jews and the ignoble Brits

While there is not ample space to deal with the whole issue of the Ashkenazi "Zionist" diaspora and its accompanying controversies in depth, there is one issue, however, which, because of the backing it received from Britain and from influential Zionists in Europe, requires our attention as a subject of paramount interest.

The issue was the idea to establish a homeland in Kenya between 1902 - 1905 for those European Jews who had become victims of pogroms in Russia, Eastern and Central Europe and other parts of far-flung Eastern Europe.

Although these Ashkenazi Jews whose origins are 10,000 kms away from Africa have not been the only victims of racial prejudice and persecution worldwide, they have used the Holocaust to push the Zionism & Territorialism Agenda, today understood as a program for the Ashkenazi to push an ideology of wholesale land-grabbing and apartheid within *Palestine.* But the idea is important to remember, because in 1902 it provoked one of the most virulent reactions from the British settlers in colonial Kenya while at the same time it unraveled vituperative anti-Semitism across *white Kenya.*

The British and Boer Settlers saw themselves as owners of the land and the people, and as such did not want to share it with any other white people groups, let alone return it to the Africans. (sources: Mwangi wa-Githumo, Trans African Journal of History Vol. 22 (1993), pp. 87-99). It is thus interesting to note that the book, *Facing Mount Kenya* was written by a formerly uneducated man who declared passionately in a thesis that is more political than anthropological, that the very lands the Jewish were to inherit, and thus inhabit in actuality belonged to "*a very large African tribe known as the Agi-kuyu*" – and it paid well for the same British Settlers to play into this claim. The Ashkenazi Jews were eventually dumped into Palestine in 1948.

But did these Highlands really "belong" to the Agi-Kuyu?

iv. African Empires and Greater Bantu (Wa-tu) Movements

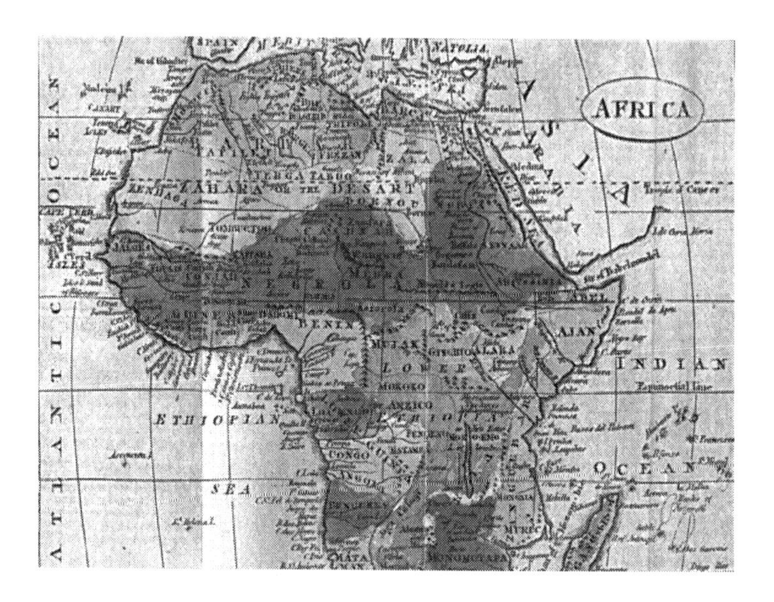

Utu movement was much more fluid than it is now, and rarely permanent apart from the cities, thus in order to find the roots of the Utu of **'Moombi'**, we would have to transverse further than what is now marked as '*Kikuyu*-land' and that the clues of the origins of the now known tribe known as *Agikuyu* would be to look for a civilization where women were warriors and ruled for over one hundred years.

African Warrior Queens

While reading the following keep in mind that historically the demise of the African Spiritual & Warrior Queen began always with the introduction of the Romano Patriarchal ideology commonly referred to as [Christianity] and formerly always disseminated by the European, be he black or white for historically the word *Caucasian* referred to a "*Black skinned inhabitant of Europe*". Whites were described as *Slavic, Germanic or Nordic.*

In terms of physical space within Africa, the British occupied that huge piece of land from the Swahili Coast to Western Uganda, dubbed it the 'British Protectorate' and set up invisible borders. But, before this, people movements were across the whole of Africa from the Indian Ocean on the East to the Atlantic Ocean to the West of Africa. Looking for a race of Warrior Queens within our current borders is to propagate the lie for we are *Africans.* And Africa, is a *Continent.*

Geographically, in the lands to the West of the current "Kenya" and central to Africa is the lake known as *Nalubale* which means 'the lake of the Goddesses' in the Buganda Language. Further west, inland to present day West Africa, were a famous warrior tribe known as the *Mino*, which means "*our mothers*" - a **Fon** all-female military regiment of the Kingdom of Dahomey in the present-day Republic of Benin which lasted until the end of the 19th century.

This Kingdom extended to present day East Africa; it was enormous. Understand that we were dived up into small bits.

To the East were the great civilizations of Axum where women were fierce fighters and warriors, while to the North and South were the greatest of Tall Dark Warriors, the people of *Maa.* In the North these Utu were known as Egyptians/Sudanese/ from the land of Kemet who were ruled often, by great Queens, and in the South these same people built the great Kingdoms of Zimbabwe, the name which represents a contracted form of *dzimba-hwe,* which means "venerated houses" in the *Zezuru* dialect of *Shona*, and usually references chiefs' houses.

The truth is harsher yet.

Did **Moombi** and her ***10 warrior daughters exist***? Are they factual people?

Warrior Queens of Dahomey

Tassi Hangbé, daughter of King Haouegbadja

Tassi Hangbé was a stateswoman who ruled the Kingdom of Dahomey from 1708 to 1711. Her father, King Houegbadja who ruled from 1645 to 1685 as the third King of Dahomey is said to have originally started the group - which would later become 'the Mino' - as a corps of elephant hunters called the *gbeto*. The Kingdom of Dahomey was a pre-colonial African Kingdom that existed from about 1600 until 1894, when the last king, Béhanzin was defeated by the French and the country annexed into the French colonial empire. Dahomey had developed on the Abomey Plateau amongst the Fon in the early 17th century and became a regional power in the 18th century by conquering key cities on the Atlantic coast. It had an organized domestic economy built on conquest, slave labor, significant international trade with Europeans, a centralized administration, taxation systems, and an organized military. Notable in the kingdom were significant artwork, the all-female military unit, the elaborate religious practices of Vodun and the large festival of the Annual Customs of Dahomey.

During this festival which was attended by Africans from across the region, they traded *slaves* captured during wars and raids and exchanged them with Europeans for goods such as knives, bayonets, firearms, fabrics, and spirits. (Alpern, Stanley B. (1998). Amazons of Black Sparta: The Women Warriors of Dahomey (1st ed.). New York, U.S.: New York University Press.)

The Mino were rigorously trained and given uniforms. Training consisted of intense physical exercises, survival skills and learning to become indifferent to physical pain by storming acacia thorn defenses in military exercises. Control of emotional pain was taught through the execution of prisoners. Serving in the Mino offered women the opportunity to "rise to positions of command and influence" in an environment that was structured for individual empowerment. The Mino were also wealthy and held high status and began to take prominent roles in the Grand Council, debating the policy of the kingdom. From the 1840s to 1870s (when the opposing party collapsed), they generally supported peace with Abeokuta and stronger commercial relations with England, favouring the trade in palm oil above that of slaves; this set them at odds with their male military colleagues who preferred the selling of slaves.

By the mid-19th century, they numbered about 6,000 women, a third of the entire Dahomey army according to reports written by visitors. These documented reports also indicated that the women soldiers suffered several defeats.

The Mino were said to be structured in parallel with the army as a whole, with a center wing (the king's bodyguards) flanked on both sides, each under separate commanders. Some accounts note that each male soldier had a female warrior counterpart, and in an 1849/50 account by an Englishman, it was documented that the women had three stripes of whitewashed around each leg and were honored with other marks of distinction.

The women's army consisted of a number of regiments: huntresses, riflewomen, reapers, archers, and gunners. Each regiment had different uniforms, weapons and commanders. In the latter period, the Dahomean female warriors were armed with *Winchester* rifles, clubs and knives and units were under female command. An 1851 published translation of a war chant of the women claims the warriors would chant, "*as the blacksmith takes an iron bar and by fire changes its fashion so have we changed our nature. We are no longer women, we are men.*"

The Mino troops were disbanded when the kingdom became a French protectorate. According to a historian who traced the lives of almost two dozen ex-Mino, all the women displayed difficulties adjusting to life as retired warriors, often struggling to find new roles in their communities that gave them a sense of pride comparable to their former lives. Many displayed a tendency to start fights or arguments that frightened their neighbours and relatives. Between 1934 and 1942, several British travelers in Abomey recorded encounters with ex-Mino, now old women who spun cotton or idled around courtyards. The last survivor of the Dahomey Mino is thought to have been a woman named Nawi. In a 1978 interview with a Beninese historian, Nawi claimed to have fought the French in 1892. Nawi died in November 1979, aged well over 100 years.

This account is valid history regarding our African Monarchies. Why is there no visible tangible proof of a Kikuyu empire? Kings? Queens? A court? All our neighbouring tribes, from the Maa to those who lived around the Lake, to the empires of Ethiopia – all these had thriving ruling systems – but when you land in Kikuyu land, suddenly there is a deep absence of culture.

v. Traveling across Africa

In his drawing up of invisible borders across African land, the European effectively cut us off from ourselves, concentrating and ushering us into pens. Leaving those pens required permission and the permission passes became more and more difficult to obtain. Today traveling includes permissions to pass various ports or portals, and entrance fees - aka visa or Verified International Stay Approval - agreement contracts that state the nature and length of a visit. This Big Brother Mentality is disheartening and frustrating for the African traveler – and that is *exactly* the point. For if we traveled more, we would know whom we are, we would share stories, poetry, songs and writing. Our Arts, Comedies and Dances would awaken lost memories. We would remember.

The Kingdom of Akzum

In Kenya we have been taught separatism and segregation by territory, and there is an underlying hostility when entering "Kikuyu Territory" towards non-Kikuyu's, or the non-Catholic/Christian. Why this hostility, for these are new beliefs and foreign to these lands. Note that all three of the Abrahamic faiths which were founded most recently in North and Northeast Africa profoundly affect and relate largely to the people of Africa – these are the Christian, Judaism, and the Islamic faiths. In the 3,000 years before the *white* person came into Africa, there were two journeys that Africans undertook and have been taking since the beginning of time –

one was to Jerusalem, known by its pre-biblical name ***Uru-Salim***, and the other annual journey was to *Mecca.* Both these annual trips were entirely based on trade & commerce. However, on this side of the common era, as we have been 'informed' by the colonizer man - our ancestors apparently travelled to these cities to worship our "gods". The word *Mecca* means "*a large marketplace – a meeting place for trade*" while ***Uru-salim*** means the "foundation of the god Shalim" - the Canaanite god of the setting sun and the nether world, as well as of health and perfection.

Other places where we as Africans often travelled to was Timbuktu, that city which harbored all the paramount learning institutions worldwide and well-placed smack bang, in the heart of Africa. Timbuktu was built in 1100AD with the Sankore Mosque being built by Al-Qadi Aqib ibn Mahmud ibn Umar, the Supreme Judge of Timbuktu in 989 AD. [A Supreme Judge or in today's language, CJ 1 or Chief Justice of the Supreme Court]. According to African scholar Shamil Jeppie in *The Meanings of Timbuktu*: Timbuktu is a repository of history, a living archive which anybody with a concern for African history should be acquainted with. Timbuktu City played an essential role as a centre of scholarship under the Songhay state until an invasion from the rulers of Marrakesh in 1591, and even thereafter it was revived. The city of Alexandria had the greatest of Libraries, but this was burnt down by Roman Julius Caesar in 48BC.

Journeying across Africa was often by camel caravan while the wealthy traveled by horse. There are thousands of images across Africa that show both male and female warriors on horses, while Queens and Kings rode Elephants. One of the most famous stories is told of Mansa Musa, the King of Mali who traveled for Pilgrimage to Mecca. Another is the Queen of Sheba aka Makeda, who traveled from her lands which included present day Yemen, to Uru-Salim when Solomon had built a magnificent temple there. From the interior of what was known as Central Africa beyond the great lakes, to the North through the Sudan, there were trade routes to *Lamu*, and to *Manbaça/ Manbasa/ or Mvita*, the last derived from *Shehe Mvita.* Meanwhile within *Tanganika* there were various Trade Routes to *Bagamoyo, Dar-es-Salaam, and Kilwa Kisiwani.*

In Ethiopia, the Christian faith embodies the man Yeshua, as a holy **black** African man and one of *their ancestors.* Christianity in Ethiopia dates to the ancient Kingdom of Aksum, when the King Ezana first adopted the faith, as Kings and Queens frequently travelled to *Uru Salim.* The largest pre-colonial Christian church of Africa was the Ethiopian Church which had a membership of between 40 and 46 million people. Having no outside influence, the persona of Yeshua is stubbornly African, and the Ethiopians persistently embrace this knowledge.

In Yemen's Sana'a in 1901, a white German man 'discovered'? a group of pure Sephardic African Jews that had not received any exterior influence. Yet Europeans made constant "assumptions" (a thing that is accepted as true or as certain to happen, without proof - a knowledge which is based on theory) that these lands had all been "ravaged" by Muslims, and that Muslims, Christians or Jews could not exist together peacefully - but we DO, to date.

However, in Kenya our founding father held firmly to and

broadcast the lie that "we" – the Kikuyu and essentially all Kenyans, were a static non-traveling group of people who have no history outside of the *Facing Mount Kenya* thesis. The myth becomes a simpletons story, not founded on facts, but written as a "fairy story". This psychology is fairly simple. When a government cages a people physically they become dumb because Big Brother can limit whatever information goes into the cage. Make travel difficult, expensive and unobtainable to the common masses, impose strict rules. This is why the British stopped Kenyans in Eastern Africa from traveling. When we compare the above historical truths to Kenyan history, we find that much of Kikuyu culture is not only confused and obscure but that stories from different families do not match up. Further there are no artifacts, no drawings, no art, no music, no talent, no true knowledge of their lands, no Kings and surprisingly for AFRICA, no lineage of Queens outside of **Moombi,** and even then, she was portrayed as a domesticated "housewife".

PART IV

In the Desert Sands of Sudan there are more pyramids than neighboring Egypt. The Nubian temples in *Dangeil* or *Meroe* are a part of the last Nubian Kingdom 300 BC–AD 300. They are built of granite and sandstone. These pyramids were partially demolished by Italian Giuseppe Ferlini in the 1830's. He was a combat medic who turned 'explorer' and later 'treasure hunter'. I have read many times and listened to accounts that stated that white Europeans, unable to conceive that ancient statues and buildings in Africa clearly portrayed 'a black advanced civilization' often became enraged and destroyed much of Africa's cities, burning, looting and taking even clothes to their museums as 'treasures'.

In recent times we have seen a return of many of these statues and treasures being returned to African states. We had a culture and a civilization. The wording 'cradle of civilization' means that all civil living began in Africa, yet 500 years ago, Europeans were quick to claim that they had brought Africans civility. Which civility?

i. A Writing Culture

Africans have been writing for over 5,000 years, but the general African public and even *scholars* of African literature are often unaware of these early literatures, believing that African literature starts in the late 1950s as the *result* of colonization. In this view, Africa is a savage Caliban who is introduced to writing by a European Prospero and *Things Fall Apart* is his first articulation! Western historians *assume* that whatever writing happened to be done on the continent was not done by Africans or in African languages and scripts - until very recently, and even then with much skepticism. This lack of awareness of the three thousand years of African writing is particularly surprising given the legions of pre-twentieth-century African texts that historians have uncovered and studied in the past fifty years! Yet the African public has not been educated!

While historians labor to overturn long-held misconceptions about Africa as a place "without history", literary critics from Europe have done little to own up to their historians assumptions of Africa as a place without literature. To date, history textbooks do not mention the libraries of Timbuktu and Alexandria, the reading and writing culture of those on the Swahili Coast, and the arts and architecture of Iberia. The extraordinarily rich trove of pre-twentieth century African continental literatures has yet to be written about in any depth by Euro-American literary critics, and where are the African Critics themselves? Certainly, no single book to date addresses their work at length and almost no literary essays published outside of Africa address the continental works. But ancient Africa had *many* indigenous scripts including *hieroglyphs* and *hieratic*, both developed in Egypt around five thousand years ago to represent the ancient Egyptian language. Egyptians then invented *Demotic*, which was related to *Hieratic*, and *Coptic*, which was related to *Greek* and used to represent African language.

Nubians used *all* the Egyptian scripts, but also invented their own - *Meroitic*, to represent the African languages of *Meroitic* and Old Nubian. Meanwhile in North Africa and the Sahel, black non-Arab Africans invented the Libyco-Berber scripts to represent a variety of Berber (Black) languages, while East Africans invented Ethiopic or Gəʿəz, to represent the African language of Gəʿəz. Along the Swahili Coast, Kiswahili was spoken in-land as far as the Congo, as far north as Sudan, and is older than Arabic by about 700 years. In the medieval period, Black Indigenous Africans in East, West, and North Africa used the Arabic script, but in the early modern period, Africans invented Ajami, which is related to the Swahili - Arabic script, for both their East and West African languages. It is only in the twentieth century that the Roman alphabet came to be used widely in Africa, and local languages were banned in Mission Schools. (adapted, Wendy Laura Belcher Early African Literature: An Anthology of Written Texts from 3000 BCE to 1900 CE)

"East Africa, so far as it received attention in the early nineteenth century **was counted as part of the Muslim World and from these limits Islam has not receded** - from the coastal shores of the Indian Ocean and past the Great Lakes Region into the Kingdom of the Buganda. There is no single *Islam culture* without literacy. Before the European penetration into South and East Africa, the peoples in these parts might have been classified either as 'military and pastoral' or 'agricultural and industrial' – with a prejudice against tillage which still persists in some parts of East and South Africa. The Great Lakes Plateau consists of an average elevation exceeding 3,000 feet. It is a region of distinctive physique in the geography of Africa. With it the neighboring ocean littoral is to be included, for cultural and commercial association with the interior highland, are intimate." -

(AFRICA, a Social, Economic and Political Geography of its Major Regions", 1934, Walter Fitzgerald)

In other words, there existed a vibrant *trade* right across Africa, and East Africa was central to this trade. There were also clear caravan routes to both "military & pastoral" as well as "agricultural & industrial" communities, and along the coast, there were populations which spoke a distinct language - *Kiswahili* – which penetrated the inland as far as Western Congo and to the shores of the Atlantic Ocean! Africa was a vibrant continent!

If one was to take *Facing Mount Kenya* at face value with Kenyatta on the cover dressed in a coarse Raymonds Wool blanket caressing a crude spear, it portrays the people of East African as illiterate and as fanciful as the '*native*' characters found in the Tarzan & Jane novels. *Tarzan of the Apes* tells the story of *Tarzan* – meaning "White Skin" in *ape language*, who is adopted as a baby by the she-ape Kala after his parents, the Lord and Lady Greystoke pass away after being marooned in West Africa!! The Tarzan books were printed first in 1912, and Jomo Kenyatta's thesis was published in 1938. Note that while his cover had him dressed in a blanket, he himself, never dressed like that in either Kenya or in London!! Throw in the fact that his cover was unlike the many pictures we see of Kings and Queens across Africa a few years before his book was written – in palaces, seated on Thrones, richly garbed and approached by the European who had to make obeisance. In his book this entire plateau elevated from 3,000ft and above sea level is formed from a seemingly isolated "dark-ages uncivilized group of savage, illiterate communities" an idea that both the Kikuyu and British often thrust at other Kenyans, with them belonging to a hierarchy of the 'most civilized'.

ii. One Utu

This is why Kenyans have cognitive dissonance when presented with historical facts - e.g., that the *waPemba* and those who lived along the East African Coast boasted of stone and coral buildings – of double and triple story homes, of fine beautifully built masjids decorated with porcelain tiles and precious stones. Of indoor toilets. Of plumbing. Of women wearing gold filigree and clothes made of silk, of wearing shoes, of hot water baths, of a culture of the arts, of poetry, music, dance, reading and *writing*. The Swahili boasted of using porcelain cutlery, slept on beds with silk sheets and cotton filled pillows, and had intermarriages with the Chinese, Omani and Indians, spoke several languages fluently, including Mandarin and Arabic. Each Masjid had a madrassa, where both male and female students went to study.

Further inland, the Kingdom of the Buganda was a fully-fledged kingdom with all of the political ramifications of any modern civilized nation. The early *Luo-Abasuba* who settled in Mfangano and Rusinga in South Nyanza were originally *Abakunta* from Buganda Kingdom. They fled to "Kenya" in 1797 after killing Kabaka Jjunju, the 26th King of Baganda. *(Ayot, H. Okello (1979). A History of the Luo-Abasuba of Western Kenya: From A.D. 1760-1940. Kenya Literature Bureau).* In Western Kenya, Uganda and Tanzania, there are accounts written by white observers of "Ugandan" doctors performing C-Sections on mothers in the 1800's, with both mother and child surviving. Same **Utu**.

In Ethiopia, there was Menelik II [17 August 1844 – 12

December 1913], an Emperor in 1889 to his death in 1913, and the Negus or King of Shewa from 1866–89 who was remembered for leading Ethiopian troops against Italy in and winning the Battle of Adwa. Why is it that as we approach the town of Muranga, when we come to central Kenya through the eyes of Jomo, history fizzles out entirely and we turn into a people without any historical past?

iii. The 9 Strangers - an investigation

Let us try and answer this other question… whom were the 'handsome men' and what were their origins? By elimination, these men were not of the of Eastern Africa Highlands which we now know extended from the Northern highlands of Axum, stretched to the Great Lakes Region, past present-day Uganda to the Congo and ended just below Lake Malawi in present day Tanzania.

In the 1950's, History taught that the Kikuyu are stated to be kin to the Congolese. But my great grandmothers stories led me to believe that the first Kikuyu were known as the *Gumba*, a small tribe of extremely dark short men who dwelled in caves. Other tales on the 'origins' of the Kikuyu include being related to the *Mijikenda* as they wandered from Middle Africa. One thing is clear – the Kikuyu did not originate from these lands as according to the fable they were "strangers and unknown" to both ***Gikoyo***, ***Moombi*** and the 10 Warrior Sisters. By horseback, it would take a less than a week to travel around Mount Kenya, a bit more, to travel to the Great Lakes Region. Note that there is no culture of agri-culture at this point.

In doing a study on the people of *Lamu* I came across the

history of a Chinese ship that had crashed on the coral reefs of one of the smaller outlying islands known as *Paté*. There, in a village of stone huts set amongst dense mangrove trees, a number of elderly men said that that they were descendants of Chinese sailors, shipwrecked on *Paté* many centuries ago. *Their ancestors had traded with the local Africans, who had given them among other gifts, zebras and giraffes to take back to China*; On this particular journey, their Ship was driven onto the nearby reef and was unable to be repaired. The sailors asked if they could stay and marry the daughters, of which the Elders agreed – but on one condition, that they must first convert to Islam in order to marry the Lamu daughters. The difference between the above story and that of the *Kikuyu* is the storyline – it is historical fact that can be proven while the Kikuyu myth is an obscure and deliberately ambiguous one.

iv. I'rua - FGM & the Trauma of Pain

Further along the book, we are pounded but not surprised with Kenyatta's arguments in favour of female circumcision that reflected theories of functionalism, a branch of social anthropology commenced – *coincidentally*– (at this point I am allowed to be sarcastic) by his Professor Malinowski, which views rituals in terms of the social functions they perform. Female circumcision, also known as clitoridectomy or, in today's more politicized language **FGM** aka female genital mutilation - was practiced in Kenya's 1930s – but by only 21% of the Kikuyu. Despite the low numbers, Kenyatta defended, insisted on and pushed FGM in the name of supporting the principle of "age-grading" (the organization of society around age-groups) as a tool for education, and particularly for teaching endurance. The larger context in which this question arose, however, was around the rights of native Africans to practice "their traditions" (note: *this by Malinowski*). Hence, in the second edition of *Facing Mount Kenya*, the subtitle of Kenyatta's thesis changed from "tribal life" to "traditional life of the *Gikuyu*."

Yes, I got hung up a lot on the sentence where Jomo *defended FGM as a tool for education and particularly for teaching endurance* - what endurance do you teach through FGM?

The debate on female circumcision (known locally as *i'rua* – from the word *ruo– aatuurirũo* pain/painful/tear apart) became heated in 1929 when the mission Church of Scotland in Kenya **banned** the practice, and furthermore required all of its members to pledge the same. Kenyatta was already in London when this ban took place, but he was livid. Note that the Kikuyu Central Association KCA membership was entirely male, and as the General Secretary, he retaliated by taking a stand in favour of FGM. What was going on in his head? Can I state that his stance on FGM was informed by a political allegiance and a position against dominance by first the church, and then the Crown?

Kenyatta had two ambitions in writing his thesis - to regain the lands lost that the son's-in-law had stolen from the *Daughters of Mombi* - by all means necessary – back from the white man and, to make sure that the **Moombi** daughters were in constant *I'rua* and thus unable to regain control of their lands. Remember that the daughters even in old age were physically stronger than the men, and well-disciplined in the arts of war and combat.

FGM has been scientifically proven to be singularly the most excruciating cutting performed on a female. In the pain meter scale where broken femurs, cluster headaches, shingles and toothaches are identified as 'the most painful experiences' that a human can suffer - FGM is 4,000% more painful. It is so painful, that it destroys the female psyche and cripples a female soul - for life. It degrades her body and kills her spirit. *Infibulation* or *pharaonic* circumcision is the "sewn closed" category which involves the removal of the external genitalia and encourages fusion of the wound. The inner and/or outer labia are cut away. Worse, it causes fistula and agonizing pain when birthing, as the vulva are absent, and there is scarring where the muscles become inflexible and hard, thus unable to dilate for birth. The condition where the bottom of the vagina wall rips a hole through to the anal wall during birth when the baby cannot naturally emerge from the vagina is known as *Fistula.*

FGM is a *curse.*

And it's history is rooted in **Rome**.

When the tribal branch of Europeans known as **Roma** first arrived in Rome during the period known as the **Byzantine Empire,** they divided themselves up as those who had direct linkages and ancestry from the gods, and those men and women who were mortal, thus doomed to a life of servitude and poverty. So great and mighty where these Elitists, that they named themselves 'Blue Bloods' on account of the colour of their veins seen through their pale strangely white skin.

Slaves were not allowed to bear children of 'the gods', and babies born from these unions were thrown to the wild wolf packs that roamed outside the city. Later it became easier to control the woman's sexuality via FGM. FGM in its severest form (*infibulation*) is where the vaginal opening is also sewn up leaving only a small hole for the release of urine and menstrual blood. Other female slaves had fibulae (brooches) pierced through their labia to prevent them from getting pregnant. Salima Ikram, professor of Egyptology at the American University in Cairo notes that "…a widespread assumption places the origins of female genital cutting in *pharaonic* Egypt. This would be supported by the contemporary term '*pharaonic* circumcision', and while there's evidence of male circumcision in Old Kingdom Egypt, there is *none* for females. This was not common practice in ancient Egypt. There is no physical evidence in mummies, neither is there anything in the arts nor literature…"

FGM and Eunuchism were both introduced as a *slave* methodology, where thousands of young boys and girls would be marked as 'ready to be sold' to the **Roma**. The girls were often identified by a thick gold anklet that could not be removed - this marked them as *slaves.* Remember that being African in itself did not mean *slavery* until the introduction of the Atlantic Slave trade. Prior to this, Africans and the Black persona were recognized as literate and equal to all human races worldwide. Thus it was necessary to mark those that were *Slaves.* Further, within that capacity, there were specific frameworks regarding the treatment of a traded servant. The ideology was that a baby/child who had their reproductive organs removed would be a *servant for life*, unable to have sexual intercourse nor bear children, and able to fetch a higher price at the markets. Male children who had their phallus removed were marked with either gold earrings or a gold nose ring. These markings were for the same purpose –

to distinguish and identify those children who could be traded as far away as Europe. When we observe particularly the Histories of Europe and of the Middle and Far East, we realize that many of these Slaves had no "families" of their own – even where they were loyal and elevated in many fiefdoms across Europe and Asia – they remained "single".

v. Timelines of The Betrayal

1. The Land 2. Ownership 3. Authority 4. Balance

After the role reversal and the revolt by the men, there was a loud cry by women across the lands. A cry, of betrayal. It has been scientifically proven that Cortisol, a natural drug in our bodies, released during deep emotional pain, will affect an infant's growth. Cortisol can elevate the blood pressure and the heart rate, increase blood sugar, and interrupt digestive and kidney functions. Infants are likely to develop when older, high levels of drug dependency, depression, lack of attention (ADD) aggression, bullying and mental health problems such as Bi-Polar and Schizophrenia. (M.R. Gunnar, "Quality of care and buffering of neuroendocrine stress reactions: potential effects on the developing human brain," *Prev Med* 27, no. 2 (Mar-Apr 1998): 208-11.)

1. The Land

Ownership of the Lands meant care, for "…according to the Tribal Legend, we are told that in the beginning of things, when mankind began to populate the earth, the man *Gikuyu*, the founder of the tribe was called by the **Mogai** – the Divider of the Universe – and was given as his share the land, ravines, the rivers, the forests, the game, and all the gifts that **Mogai** bestowed on Mankind…" - in understanding etymology, it is important to notice language flow and descriptive words. Kenyatta's use of the words 'divider' 'his share' and 'the game' (not animals) points to a language that is both rigid and *not* belonging to an African genre. In his texts concerning the ownership of the lands, Kenyatta fails to understand the context of African land ownership - that the land cannot be owned by *man*, that land belongs to a community and requires a balance of maintenance, sustenance and nourishment, and that the land had been in the care of the 10 sisters plus their Mother for a period of at least 100 years. In a single week, the care of the land was overturned. So too was the army. It was a coup d'état extraordinaire, only that a problem immediately arose.

2. Ownership

As the women sank into their pain of betrayal, a cry spread throughout the lands, and there was a noticeable absence - there were no women warriors to take care of the land. For had not the men taken over that mantle? Abruptly, in less than a week, the women were bullied to stay at home and cook, (is this why the *Daughters of Moombi* are abysmal cooks?) while the men rode out…but to do what? In their planning to overthrow their women, they in fact, made a blunder. Where the women outriders had kept the foreigner at bay, where they had a system that worked, the Kikuyu men let the white colonizer into the center of the lands, whereupon history shows that the newly self-named *Gikuyu* men lost the same lands that they had conned their women out of. Towards the end of the 19th century, Muranga and Thika fell into the hands of the foreign white European.

The sins of the fathers passed onto the sons, and the land

issue become an obsession to a group of middle-aged Kikuyu men who when as young boys and teenagers, had witnessed the passage of female land ownership into their old fathers' hands – through treachery. But one thing was clear – women could not be allowed to regain control of the lands. In their treachery, the men self- defeated themselves, but refused to admit that they had made a serious error, and further, instead of attending to the wrongs that their fathers committed against their mothers, these men, together with Johnstone Kamau devised a diabolic campaign that began with the law that women should be circumcised to weaken them further. Johnstone Kamau hyped up this propaganda through the KCA who had offices in Muranga, Thika, Embu and Meru – the Mount Kenya Region.

3. Authority

Female Warriors and Keepers of the Land

There were 10 daughters. Warrior Queens of Moombi.

The lands had been given to the Daughters of Moombi for a reason as ordained by **Mogai** – they held the Banner of Protection of the Lands against it's physical, mental and spiritual destruction. These 10 daughters had grown and been trained in the wholesome care of the lands. Each had a specific name which symbolized the systemic cultural structures that both reflected and instructed their sacred duties. These 'houses' were 'schools' where children were taught disciplines.

(I) Acheera; Travellers, knowledge gatherers, storytellers

(2) Agachiko; Marketers, negotiators, wise – dealers with

outsiders in terms of trade

(3) Airimo; Healers, shamans, diviners, seers

(4) Amboi; Defenders of the lands and song Leaders – especially when going to war

(5) Angare of Wildlife – trackers (the art of reading signs in the bush)

(6) Anjiro; Mystical and possessing spiritual powers. Defenders and offer sacrifices for warriors before war

(7) Angoi; Goddesses: Overseers of the entire lands – environment and people – leaders

(8) Ethaga; Rain makers and healers – shamans, sages, very Spiritual

(9) Aitherando: Lovers of Humans, Justice and Law, bringers of spiritual balance and order – "Ka" in Africa and also known as "Chi" in the East

(10) Wamuyu: - Life. Both Spirit and physical, holds the entire lands together. Also known as **Warigia**, she remained single as a choice. However, she 'adopted' her sisters children, those who felt they wanted to remain set apart, i.e., – single – as seers.

Mogai had given the mantle to The Daughters to protect the land, and in doing so bequeathed them with "…all the *gifts* that the Lord of *Nature* bestowed..."

4. Balance

The Etymology of Language and Things

Let us go back to the name of the 'lands'. According to Jomo Kenyatta's *Facing Mount Kenya, 'Gikuyu'* was told to settle with his wife *Moombi*– the 'Creator' in a place known as Mokorwe wa Nyagathanga which means "the place of "fig trees" and the bird species 'nyagathanga'. It is to be noted that the fig tree is common to the whole of sub-Saharan Africa, and are sacred trees to *all* Bantu peoples, each whom have a name for the fig tree – this tree it is *not* peculiar to 'Kikuyu' tribe, although Jomo Kenyatta deliberately presented it as existing only among the Kikuyu and only special to the Kikuyu, disregarding the function of the tree throughout the other provinces of Kenya and indeed of Africa. In fact, the fig tree is so proliferated in Africa that it is the most common tree, followed by the Acacia. Considering that this book was written in 1938 – it was appalling clear that the greatest of all trees, the fig tree, grew across the continent. How could Kenyatta *not know* this?

This Bird species 'nyaga thanga' is recorded as 'unknown' by the Kikuyu. Yet when one considers the word in *Utu* and in Egyptian Hieroglyphics, it comes from the word *'anga'* – the definition being 'Juu', also 'Wingu', 'Mbingu' and 'Uwingu' – Nya ga-anga – literally meaning "of the heavens" and is not a 'bird' flapping about in the sky but implicates a physical land. **Mogai** showed to *Gikuyu* a land full of 'the fig tree of the heavens' - heaven being not an obscure place in the sky as denoted by theology, but a real place on earth according to the Bantu. And this physical land had been handed down to the 10 daughters and their female descendants as proscribed by **Mogai**, a god whom one faced in the general direction of Mecca, for if you stand in the area Muranga or Thagana today, and lift up your hands 'facing Mount Kenya', one shall directly face the same direction as Muslims face when praying (that's a sidebar). The handsome strangers were to assist in this *proliferation* and to live balanced ordered lives, in accordance with a *proscribed* pattern set out by **Mogai.**

In the old **Gikoyo** language, women were collectively known as *Aka*, derived from the verb - *gũaka* – to *create, invent, craft, design, form.* Not coincidentally, this is the name of The *Moombi*, the First Woman. She was '*Creator & Moulder*'. In popular myths, *Moombi* was not directed to worship **Mogai**, for she herself was a goddess who had the gift of creation which she passed onto her daughters - but not to her sons. The children *could not be called the children of Gikoyo* for he could not create and he *had* to pray, sacrifice and raise his hands towards **the Mountain**, which he did, diligently.

Life was balanced. The Stranger sons by marriage were known in plural as 'andu a nja' meaning 'people from outside' and in the singular form 'mũtumia' which in gikoyo means "the one who remains silent", while the word 'Mutumia' even today amongst the Kamba means 'a man'.

After the revolt, both the terms 'andu a nja' and 'mutumia' came to convey the term *woman.* How is this? Let me answer myself - the men reversed the natural **Mogai** given roles. This exposes another thread – that although the women were the creators, the strangers who were truly 'from outside' turned around and renamed the female 'andu a nja'.

So deeply has this story of *Facing Mount Kenya* been ingrained into Kikuyu hierarchy that few women have a standpoint in the current Kikuyu patriarchal system, and they lag behind their sisters in other parts of the country. While it is not rare to find strong Kikuyu women - because they fight tooth, nail and natural hair for their rights - even then there is the stain of disdain and rejection from an extremely high percentage of "educated" Kikuyu men. In Kenya, women's human rights are frequently addressed by non-kikuyu males.

There is a tribe of the Amazon forest in Columbia known as the *Tukanoans*. They believe that God created man, but not woman. Woman, they believe, already existed in the form of Earth – "Earth is a womb, all life forms are planted in the womb of Mother Earth. She protects and nourishes every life form. A woman's womb represents the fluid earth. Seeds swim in that fluid until they germinate. Humans swim until birth." How can we plant in a womb which has an imbalance of energies? Rain alone cannot give us a future. The sun, the moon, the soil, ancestors, the unborn, wind, insects, trees, rivers, fire, animals, and volcanoes – all are living, cosmic energies." (*Kariuki wa Thuku, The Sacred Footprint, Vol 1, A Story of Karima Sacred Forest, towards reclaiming of the Community Territorial Stewardship of Natural and Cultural Heritage.*)

Woman. I can see the wheels in your mind turning…

Woman. I can see the wheels in your mind turning…

Kenyan woman, how can we **plant** in a land which has an imbalance of energies?

PART V

We as Kenyans in particular, have been lied to for the tribe known as "Kikuyu" did NOT exist before the 1800's. Further there is no land that is "Kikuyu Land" because as a tribe, they did not exist.

i. Lies, The Kikuyu, Kenyans & Politics

"Vururi uyo ni wiito"

How often do Kikuyu's chant this slogan amongst themselves? It is stated casually, like a tiny raindrop from an otherwise blue sky that is cloud free – but it is akin to an acidic chemical burn to those who are not "Kikuyu". Translation should be impossible, yet many Kikuyu spit this phrase in the face of all others – unapologetic and superior. "We fought for this land!" – they state when asked why they think that Kenya belongs to Kikuyu only, alone… "…the Mau Mau were The Kikuyu and the founding father was Mau Mau and he led the REVOLT and secured freedom from the mzungu for us!" Propaganda?

Jomo Kenyatta was never a member of the *Mau Mau*, nor did he lift a finger to fight in any war. Yet, "…..the Kenyatta family alone today own about 17.5% of Kenya's 25% of arable land." (Ibid). Within the Kikuyu tribe itself is a cartel known as The Mount Kenya Mafia who make up less than 1.5% of the total Kenyan population. It is they whom own the rest of the arable land, with a majority of 45 million Kenyans owning less than a quarter of an acre or no land at all, thus regulating them to an eternal serfdom in a country where living off the land is the only means of survival. Those who own land often buy land through Banks or Land Credit Loan corporations which are in turn owned by the Kenyatta family, by relatives, or by close friends of this "ruling family", usually members of the 'Elite Class' - and an extension of the Mount Kenya Mafia.

Jomo Kenyatta achieved his goal. He not only acquired the lands of the 10 daughters, but he also went ahead and looted all the land that was illegally allocated to the British Protectorate, evicting millions and causing a singular phenomenon known as IDP – a people who are homeless and landless in their own country or Internally Displaced Persons. No, do not even begin to lie that people were returned to their lands or given 'new lands' for they were not.

ii. Branding, Advertising and Propaganda

Our first presidents' given name is Kamau and not Kenyatta. During the First World War, Johnstone Kamau as he was then called, ran away from his home to avoid being conscripted into the British Army – thousands of those who were called "Kikuyu Tribe" were a part of this Army and FOUGHT for the British, but Kamau in his characteristic cowardly manner, fled. The Maasai in their superior honesty had adamantly refused to be conscripted into the British Army, and it is to the Maasai that cowardly Johnstone fled and lived with the family of an aunt who had married a Maasai chief, laying 'low', adopting Maasai customs and wearing Maasai jewelry to avoid detection. His disguise including a Maasai beaded belt known as a *kinyata* in the Kikuyu language. This is when he took to calling himself *Kinyata* which he anglicized to *Kenyatta* while in London. Would he have named himself "*Kenyarra*" if he was in the United States of America?

In present day advertising there is a term known as **Branding**. It involves heavy research and tests the populace for acceptance of new ideas. In a paper written by Jonathan A.J. Wilson in October 2013 entitled **Science and Branding** or the 'Science of Branding', he argues that 21st century marketing marks the dawn of an age that surpasses simple industrialization, commerce, and structuralism, and celebrates more human traits. Financial and economic interactions are the culmination of human transactions in the widest sense, transactions which begin with exchanges of thoughts, emotions, experiences, and social activities. Therefore, this 'Marketing' is spearheaded by 'Branding,' which represents the acceptance and harnessing of paradoxical, oxymoronic, allegorical, metaphorical, and esoteric tensions in culture, emotion and spirituality.

Were the creators of **Brand Kenya** ahead of their times, for branding is an important and basic function of human existence. At a conference on Consumer Culture Theory held at Oxford Saïd Business School, Beth DuFault and James McAlexander presented a paper, part of therein that stated, "By researching primary source documents, we demonstrate that Newtonian science and the birth of what we now know as the scientific method itself achieved acceptance, in part, owing to the activities of Isaac Newton and his advocates that can be best described as marketing. The successful diffusion of the Newtonian scientific belief system was influenced by marketing activities that included a) promotion, b) sales of representatives c) demonstrative products, and d) publicity. These marketing activities worked to build the equity of the Newtonian Brand and to overcome the competitive offerings of the time."

The Science of Branding has always been around us but – just like "Intel" – a sticker had to be placed on the outside of the vehicle for it to receive attention and mass consideration. Politicians have been using the Science of Branding for thousands of years, with a well-placed spokesperson who is often the orator or the Spokesman of the Brand. Branding is about the human experience and is a fundamental function of human existence, and in politics it is a tool better known as **propaganda**. *Facing Mount Kenya*, according to scholar Simon Gikandi, was "one of the major texts in what has come to be known as the invention of tradition in colonial Africa".

Despite the **KCA** being "fervently" and ruthlessly against the Church and Crown, both maintained their vampiric presence in Kenya through the conniving support of Jomo Kenyatta. Neither the Church nor the Crown that he had stood so firmly against were repulsed from Kenya, nor were the massive parcels of lands they had possessed during colonization confiscated. By the time he died, none of the lands that had been confiscated by the British, not even a single acre, had been returned to the original indigenous people.

Kenyatta himself was crowed and celebrated as the first the Prime Minister of Kenya, then later as President of Kenya, despite his never being *Mau Mau,* nor a revolutionary. His speeches were written for him by a team, his orations were as emotionally powerful as those of Barak Obama. Kenyan's needed a hero. They got a Trojan Horse.

Kenyatta also appeared in thousands upon thousands of pictures from about 1914 to 1963, pictures taken by a British Press, for fellow Africans could not owe such equipment and many were largely disinterested in Johnstone Kamau. African Black journalists back then did not even exist within the Kenyan Media Structure, so who was calling the shots of adulation? When the British charged him and five senior KAU members with masterminding the *Mau Mau*, the historian John M. Lonsdale stated that Kenyatta had been made a "scapegoat", while A. B. Assensoh later suggested that the authorities "knew very well" that Kenyatta was not involved in the *Mau Mau*, but that they were nevertheless committed to silencing his calls for an independent *Kikuyuland.*

So "disliked" was he by the "Europeans" that when the "Kapenguria 6" were jailed, he was "separated" from them for his own safety for "…a plot to murder him was uncovered…". In truth, Kenyatta was hated by his fellow Kenyans for the arrest, torture and death of Field Marshal Dedan Kimathi who was the true brilliant well-spoken, well-read leader of the *Mau Mau.* So, is all this coincidence or was it just a brilliant propaganda campaign to fan the flames of his so-called nonexistent popularity? For in 1958, Rawson Macharia, one of the key witness in the state's prosecution of Kenyatta, signed an affidavit swearing that his evidence against Kenyatta had been false - this was widely publicized and the imprisoned Kenyatta suddenly become a symbol of "African Nationalism" across the continent. That's what the "media" says. FM Dedan Kimathi meanwhile was "caught" tried and hanged in 1957, and to date, Kenyans have no idea where the body of this hero lies.

His sentence served; Kenyatta was released from Lokitaung in April 1959. The administration then placed a "restricting order" on Kenyatta. He went to live in Lodwar and was 'forced' to report to the DC twice a day. The 72-year-old Kenyatta was reunited with his wife, Ngina a 17-year-old child-bride who had been gifted to him by Kikuyu Elders in 1951. Uhuru Kenyatta, their 2nd born child, was born in October of 1961.

iii. Of Maternal Lineages and a Matriarchal Society

"A Man Cannot Bear Children" – African Proverb

A paternal lineage is impossible to record - in their wisdom, African Mothers hold their daughters children to their bosom but may be harsh with their daughter's in-law offspring. This is why it was critical to know the maternal lineage of a child. Custom also declared that taking a child from their mother will turn them into a bereft youth. What is Kenya today, but a country run by tired old men who disregard the mothers of their sons, institutionalize education before 9 years of age, then expect the same youths to respect them?

Research leads to a short dark, 'pygmy' tribe of men who lived underground in the caves of the Nyandarua Ranges and were the original occupants of that small hilly area between the southeastern flanks of the Ranges and lower and further east toward the Thagana island, today known as Muranga. They were sighted (coincidentally) only by the Gikuyu and some Ogiek peoples. This is odd, and further, according to "Kikuyu tradition", these short dark men were fierce, warlike but "backward and lacking in civility". While they were not entirely savage, they espoused the very distinctiveness of what the white European man stated he found in the area – short dark men who were agriculturalists, hunter-gathers, a sullen race of men who worked with iron, made pottery and were beekeepers. There is rarely any mention of women. Without the African fe-male, the male will die.

Moombi was not Kikuyu. **Moombi** was a "female" meaning **umbi**– a creator; which in the English language translates to "fe-male" or "womb•man". However, in understanding this concept, one must comprehend that there is no real definition of the **African Female Form** in the language of the European. In African mythology, the Black Human Female Human Form, is the beginning of all things – it is **Creator**. This was recently WikiLeaked into social media conversation away from science - and with proven parameters.

According to the genetic thread that many civilizations before us were very aware about, there is only one type of cell that is able to 'recreate' itself 'eternally', and that cell is from the womb of the Black Woman. This knowledge is often informed as untrue, false and labeled propaganda by Governments and Mass Media alike for obvious reasons. The details of the paper are far too long to add on to here, but in short, the finding of the cells was an accidental discovery.

In the 1950's, while looking for cures for diseases that besot the white man, scientists would try to find a cure through the growing of what is called "culture tissue". These experiments continually failed because the cells would die. However, cells taken from a black slave woman changed the course of modern medicine. In 1951, a scientist at Johns Hopkins Hospital in Baltimore, Maryland, "created" the first immortal human cell line with a tissue sample taken from a young black woman with cervical cancer. Those cells, called *HeLa* cells, quickly became invaluable to medical research—though their donor deliberately remained a mystery for decades.

Understand that according to The White Superiority Theory, to the Darwin Theory, and to The Theory of Eugenics, black blood is tainted. The African is a beast, uncivilized, and below the human rung. Further, according to the hedonistic patriarchal principles of the church and all Western developed, manmade-religions, the feminine form is 'the root of all evil' – sinful and beyond redemption. This belief has been deeply embedded and ingrained into a vast majority of human population, worldwide. The African Black Woman is below the African Black Man, who is already at the bottom of the human rung – in shelter, health care, education, resources, government services, in religion, in spirituality. This card has been drummed into the world psyche for such a long time that it would take years for humans to understand not only the wrongs inflicted on the African Black Female Form, but also on the implications that her Womb Cells never die.

The cell lines that medical researchers and scientists use are immortal—they can grow indefinitely, be frozen for decades, divided into different batches and shared among scientists. In her new book, The Immortal Life of Henrietta Lacks, journalist Rebecca Skloot tracks down the story of the source of the *HeLa* cells, **Madam Henrietta Lacks** herself - and documents the cell line's impact on both modern medicine and on the Lacks family. Her immortal cells are also known as STEM CELLS and were first used to grow cultures that were essential to developing the Polio vaccine. They were sent up in the first Space Missions in the USA, to see what would happen to cells in zero gravity. Many scientific landmarks since then have used this woman's cells, including cloning, gene-mapping and in vitro fertilization. Twenty-five years after Henrietta died, a scientist discovered that many cell cultures thought to be from other tissue types, including breast and prostate cells, were in fact *HeLa* cells. It turned out that *HeLa* cells could float on dust particles in the air and travel on unwashed hands and grow on other cultures! The story became an enormous controversy because these *HeLa* cells were the first human biological materials ever bought and sold and launched a multi-billion-dollar industry within the United States.

When Henrietta's destitute son discovered that American conglomerates were selling vials of their mother's cells and that the family did not get any of the resulting profits, they became, and rightly so, incensed. For Henrietta's family has lived in poverty most of their lives, could not afford health insurance nor health care while one of Henrietta sons was homeless and living on the streets of Baltimore. The family launched a campaign to right this human injustice to so as to receive benefits deserved from the sale of their own mothers cells. This is when the story of the *HeLa* cells broke, and furthermore, that cells taken from the womb of the Black African woman do not "die."

….. Back to Kenya

iv. Land Issues

According to Kenyatta's myth, Gik-uyu – **uyu** meaning 'the one', or Agik-uyu meaning "Fig" tree - together made up "one unit". Unsure of the boundaries of the land, **Mogai** took The One Man up to the highest mountain of the area and said "... – look – all this land has been made by this **Moombi** – the maker. Your home, if you stay with her, is between these 4 (four) mountains." The question floats like a feather in the air - why would **Mogai** have had to take 'The One Man' up the mountain to 'see the land'? Should he not have been aware of its boundaries? If you walk into any Borana/ Samburu/ Rendille community today, the men there within it will tell you lay of the land and the boundaries in vivid detail. If you go to the home of any man today, he will show you where his plot of land ends and begins and show you the "markers". The answer for Gik-uyu lies in a simple truth.

He would not have been aware of the boundaries of a land that did not belong to him.

And particularly not if he lived in Thagana, within the grottoes, spacious caverns & subways of the deeply forested Nyandarua Ranges. Side note: There are thousands of beautiful underground cities which are just recently being unearthed worldwide. The descriptions of "living underground" that have previously been shared by a colonial Darwinism theory evoke negative imagery of small cold mud-filled "cave" structures. In truth, underground cities were expansive, vastly beautiful, elegant, safe, scenic, and protected from top earth elements. Thousands of these cities existed in Africa (which is the largest continent on the Earth) while other underground cities and communities have been found across Europe and Asia. It is believed that the *Gumba* lived in one of these cities below Nyandarua and were iron smelters -

artisans of beautiful iron work.

Between the Nyandarua Ranges and the Kingdom of the Baganda there was only one other fierce people – the *Maasai*, hated virulently by both the White man and the Kikuyu, for they would not trade their land for money. A number of 'Kikuyu' yarns regarding land have been shamelessly plagiarized by the Kikuyu culture. Note also, that the Fig tree is proliferate across the entire lands of sub-sahara Africa - surprisingly, there are more Fig trees in the flat plains of the savannah where the cattle roam, than there are in the densely woody forests of the Ny'andarua or in the steep hills and valleys of Muranga.

v. Historical Oxymorons, Religious conflicts and Presidential Betrayals

Although it is accepted worldwide that Kenyans received "Independence" in 1963 in a land that has come to be known as **Kenya**, the Kenyatta family have used their positions to create a fiefdom where they are the sole rulers of the State of Kenya. The Rules, Customs and Laws that were written in the book *Facing Mount Kenya* were replicated by the government to grasp a fierce control of this country from its true owners. The book *Facing Mount Kenya* is a SET TEXTBOOK that must be read by every Law Student in Kenya.

The scholar Simon Gikandi commented that *Facing Mount Kenya* was "one of the major texts in what has come to be known as the invention of tradition in colonial Africa". "Caring" and nurturing of these lands is not valued under Kikuyu custom for above all, extraction is prized - where all that is on - and all that is below the land, becomes a commodity to be extracted, distributed and sold for profit. There is also a real and alarming intimacy between Johnstone Kamau and the UK Royal Family headed by Queen Elizabeth II - unlike other "black" and African families.

It is stranger yet that the *Mau Mau* whose mandate was to "kick out colonization" and return the land back to the correct owners, were banned as an entity not only by Jomo, but also by the second President Moi. Despite Jomo Kenyatta's historical claims that the *Mau Mau* rebellion freed Kenya from imperialism, none of its members as a Revolutionary Association received any lands from those they were repatriated from, and neither have they received formal historical accolades from their Government, or even financial recognition for Kenya's so-called "independence".

A Thesis, or a Kikuyu Political Manifesto?

Throughout his life, the history of Jomo Kenyatta reads as one of an opportunist selfish cowardly man. It is smoothly told, yet when one researches and begins to scratch beneath the glittery surface, the alarming truths of a puppet on a very long brutish British rope begin to unravel. For Kenyans countrywide, the knowledge that the 'lands' must all belong to the Kikuyu is no longer just alarming, it is now disturbing. Over and over again throughout this country's history is the question, why are our country laws so very unfavorably dominant?

Facing Mount Kenya was a commercial failure, selling only 517 copies. Murray-Brown later described it as "*a propaganda tour de force. No other African had made such an uncompromising stand for tribal integrity.*" The book is unpalatable to other tribes in

Kenya. Was this invention of a culture written into the book and further translated into the Laws of the Kenyan Government?

It would seem so.

Kenya's Laws are suspiciously similar to the laws of the Christian Churches, in particular the High Anglican Church and The Catholic Church of England. The land laws of Kenya The State are replicas of the laws of the Kikuyu 'tradition', which are a duplication of outdated imperial UK laws. Physically, this can be seen when African black judges in Kenya's High Court wear White wigs and an ignorant public normalizes it.

A few months ago, a young woman from London came to live and work in Nairobi. "…it's like I am not in Africa..", she said, shocked, "… this is ridiculous. This city is a carbon copy of London, I may as well be living in London, there is not a single difference…". As a well-seasoned traveler, she was startled, stating that never before had she come across a city that does not carry its own unique and distinct culture. For many a Kikuyu and the 'wannabe' set, this comparison would be one of pride.

Long before, during and after Independence, the will of the late Kenyatta became dominant across these lands without apology, while outside Kenya he was called a 'domineering prick' by leaders across Africa and was not regarded as a true revolutionary but rather as a turncoat. However, British media carefully branded his name and today he is hailed as one of the leading statesmen of Africa, a Hero of the People in Black America, in Jamaica and other former British colonies. In Africa though, he was disliked. In another city outside Kenya, I once had a startling conversation with an articulate Diplomat, formerly an Ambassador to China, who shook his head sadly when I mentioned the late Kenyatta as the founding father of Kenya, "…Kenyatta? You people have been so brainwashed! Kenyatta was a stooge for the British! A peddler! An uneducated scoundrel who was paid to divide his people ….".

He was being kind, I think.

Kenya's political history is founded on tribalism, on division, and on the concepts of capitalism. Kikuyu Culture is founded on the approbation of the Male figure, and the diminishing of the female form – the female and the feminine is rejected as superfluous, redundant and unnecessary. In Kikuyu culture the female is known as 'the person outside' - of little consequence. Her viewpoint is unnecessary. Her work, dismissed. Her input, disregarded. Her value, disdained. The Kikuyu Law regarding land upholds that only a man can sell or buy land. And that a man can only sell, or buy land, from another man. In many other cultures across Kenya, land cannot be sold for it does not belong to a single person and is inherited as communal land to care for the community in its entirety. These cultural land-laws are old guidelines that have been handed down from past generations.

The selling of land as a commodity is a concept that is not understood by 98% of a non-kikuyu population. Yet according to the Laws of the Land and between the elite and the 'learned' of Kenya and amongst the 'Kikuyu' – land is a commodity which is being sold and traded on a regular basis.

"When the European comes to the country and robs the people of their land, the white is taking away not only their livelihood, but the quantifiable symbol that holds family together. In doing this he gives blows, and these blows cut away at the foundations from the whole of Gikuyu life - social, moral, and economic. When the European explains to his own satisfaction and after the most superficial glance at the issues involved, that he is doing this for the sake of the Africans, to civilize them, to teach them the disciplinary value of regular work, and give them the benefit of European progressive ideas, he is adding insult to injury, and convinces no one but himself." (Jomo Kenyatta 1938: 305)

"When the Kikuyu, (or the white neo-colonizer), comes to the country and robs the people of their land, they are taking away not only their livelihood, but the quantifiable symbol that holds family units together. In doing this, he gives blows, and these blows cut away at the very foundations from the whole of life - social, moral, and economic. When the Kikuyu (or the White Neo-Colonialist) explains to his own satisfaction and after the most superficial glance at the issues involved, that he is doing this for the sake of the natives, to civilize them, to teach them "the disciplinary value of regular work," and give them the benefit of "Kikuyu progressive ideas", he is adding insult to injury, and convinces no one but his Kikuyu or White self."

CONCLUSION

Kenya's entire land structural laws are based on myths and fables, while the Kikuyu tribe itself has been done a great disservice regarding it's true origins. When we visit other people groups in the area, they have written accounts which are as old as 1000 years and before. The anthropological studies of any of these people groups leads to thousands of books held by older family members and grandparents. Their histories are alive with tangible proofs, old potteries, ancient houses, jewelry that is over 500 years old, items of clothing.

Facing Mount Kenya, first published in 1938, is said to be an anthropological study of the people of the Kikuyu ethnicity of central Kenya. This is a blatant lie.

Kenyatta himself states that "the cultural and historical traditions of the Gikuyu people have been orally handed down from generation to generation, but not written."

- this is such a fabulous untruth that it boggles the mind, for many texts regarding those who lived in these lands were written long before the arrival of the British. Long before! Kiswahili and Arabic *scripts* existed thousands of years before this common era/CE. Hebrew, and the Hieroglyphics we know. As Kenyans, we were not taught that the Ge'ez script of Ethiopia is the most ancient African script still in use today.

As mentioned in Part 4, other scripts are the Nsibidi of Nigeria, Adrinka of the Akan people of Ghana, the Tifnagh of the Tuareg people, and Val and Mende of Liberia and Sierra Leone, (evidence of its Liberian/Sierra Leonean age date from Goundaka, Mali that date to 3000 B.C). The oldest scripts are over 5,000 years old from the Proto Saharan region of The Sudan. Other scripts are the Aire Soroba of Mali, the Osmanya, Tifinagh, Bamum, Adlam, Bassa Vah, Medefaidrin, and N'Ko – all these African SCRIPTS are over 2,000 years old. So, when Jomo states that Kikuyu "records were not written…" we must ask the necessary questions. Why did Kenyatta lie?

We had millions of men and women who wrote. Africans had language and writing skills, poetry, and the arts. The English script is new. English is a West Germanic language that originated from Ingvaeonic languages which were taken to Britain in the mid-5th to 7th centuries AD by Anglo-Saxon migrants from what is now northwest Germany, southern Denmark, and the Netherlands. The English did not have "letters" – it is they who had no writing skills. The Table Alphabetical, the first dictionary in English was published by Robert Cawdrey in 1604 when the letter 'J' was added to Modern English.

To presume that "any group of educated intelligent Africans kept their "knowledge in their heads" is both a farce and further, a despicable principle. It assumes that only the holder of the knowledge in his head is 'right', and all else is erroneous.

Kenyatta continued,

"…. as a Gikuyu myself, I have carried them in my head for many years, since people who have no written records to rely on learn to make a retentive memory and do the work of libraries" – again, this is both poppycock and rubbish to state it lightly.

As an example, let us visit the **Njuri Ncheke**. They are the supreme governing council of elders for the Ameru peoples of Kenya. The Njuri Ncheke fill a judicial role and are at the apex of the Meru traditional judicial system and their edicts apply across the entire community. The elders forming the Njuri-Ncheke are carefully selected and comprise mature, composed, respected and incorruptible members of the community. This is necessary as their work requires great wisdom, personal discipline, and knowledge of the traditions. The Njuri Ncheke have vast libraries. I have in my work come across many councils of Elders, and all of them have ancient written records.

Why is it only the Kikuyu tribe and tribes in Kenya that don't have written records, and further why is it that our entire source of an ancient historical social system lies within the pages of that single narrow text?

Ends.

To download Facing Mount Kenya

<https://www.sahistory.org.za/sites/default/files/file%20uploads%20/jomo_kenyatta_facing_mount_kenya_the_tribal_lifbook4me.org_.pdf>.

ABOUT THE AUTHOR

Najar Nyakio Munyinyi is a passionate environmentalist, writer, African historian, and researcher. She holds a BA Design Degree, is a Certified Biophilic Design practitioner; a permaculturalist, Permaculture Gardens Designer; is locally certified as a knowledge holder of indigenous herbs, shrubs and plants for healing purposes; and is a member of Rotary International.

Nyakio resides in Nanyuki, and her bedroom window has a beautiful view facing Mount Kenya, pun intended.

Made in the USA
Middletown, DE
12 November 2024